BATIK PATTERNS

SHAMBHALA AGILE RABBIT EDITIONS

BOSTON

1999

BATIK PATTERNS

Shambhala Publications, Inc.
Horticultural Hall
300 Massachusetts Avenue
Boston, Massachusetts 02115
http://www.shambhala.com

© 1999 by Pepin van Roojen

Published in association with the Museum of Ethnology Rotterdam, The Netherlands

987654321
Printed in Singapore
∞ This edition is printed on acid-free paper that meets the American National Standards
Institute z39.48 Standard.
Distributed in the United States by Random House, Inc., and in Canada by Random House of
Canada Ltd

Library of Congress Cataloging-in-Publication Data

Batik patterns / [compiled by Pepin van Roojen].
        p.   cm.
   ISBN 1-57062-477-1 (alk. paper)
   1. Batik—Themes, motives.   I. Roojen, Pepin van.
NK9503.B38 1999
746.6'62041—dc21   99-19172
                                                            CIP

This book contains high-quality images for use as a graphic resource or inspiration. All the images are stored on the accompanying CD-ROM in professional-quality, high-resolution format and can be used on either Windows or Mac platforms. The images can be used free of charge.

The documents can be imported directly from the CD-ROM into a wide range of layout, image-manipulation, illustration, and word-processing programs; no installation is required. Many programs allow you to manipulate the images. Please consult your software manual for further instructions.

The names of the files on the CD-ROM correspond with the page numbers in this book. Where applicable, the position on the pages is indicated: T = top, B = bottom, C = center, L = left, and R = right.

Other books with CD-ROM by Shambhala Agile Rabbit Editions:

ISBN 1-57062-480-1	Chinese Patterns
ISBN 1-57062-483-6	Decorated Initials
ISBN 1-57062-478-x	Floral Patterns
ISBN 1-57062-484-4	Graphic Frames
ISBN 1-57062-479-8	Images of the Human Body
ISBN 1-57062-482-8	Sports Pictures
ISBN 1-57062-481-x	Transport Pictures

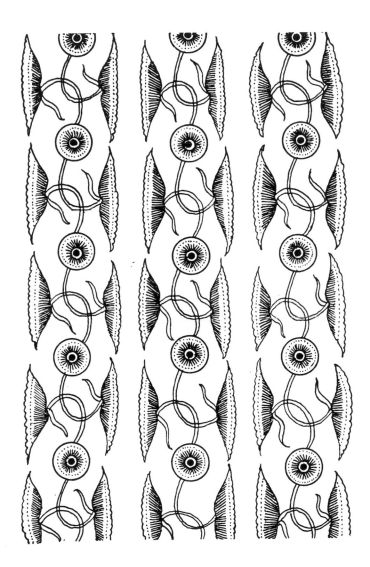

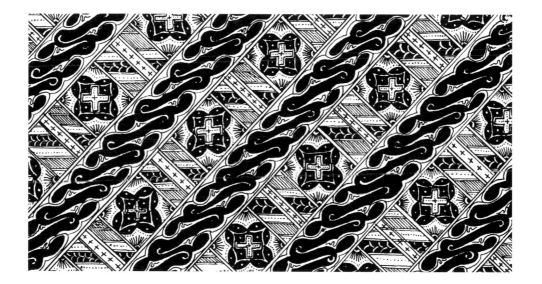

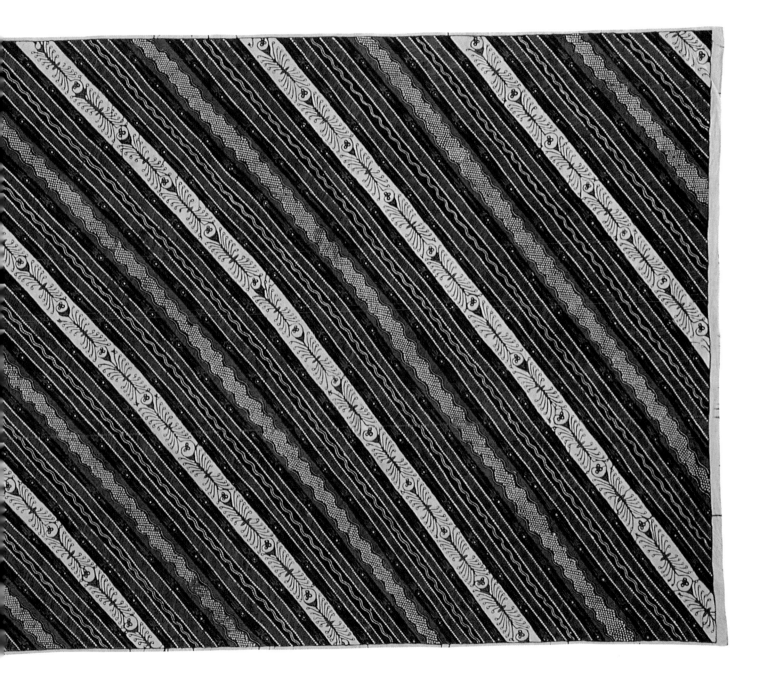

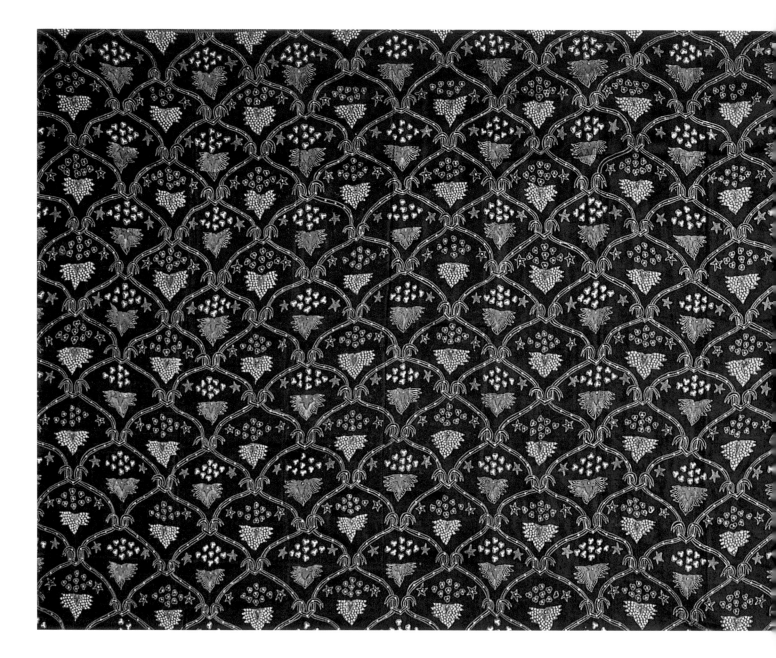

44

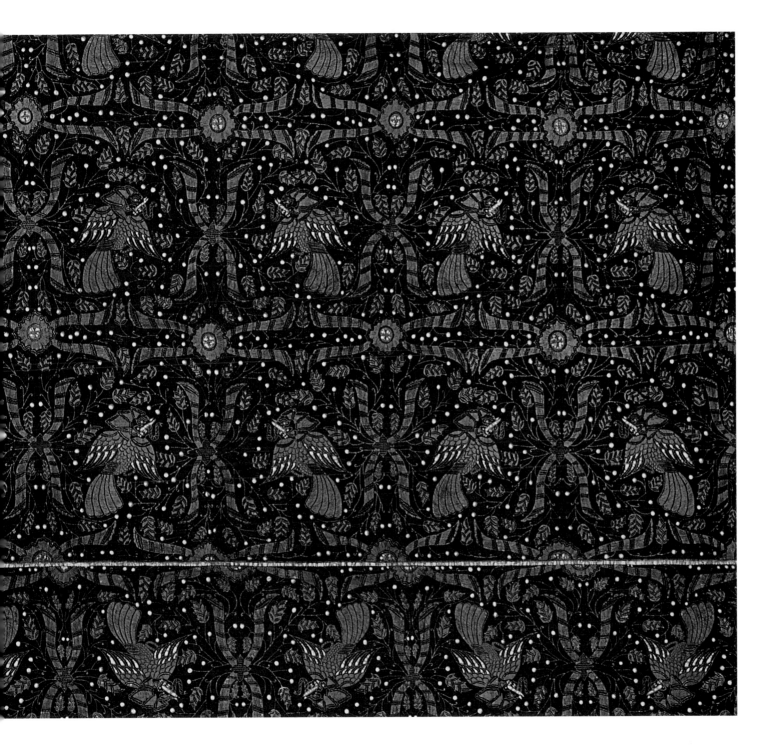

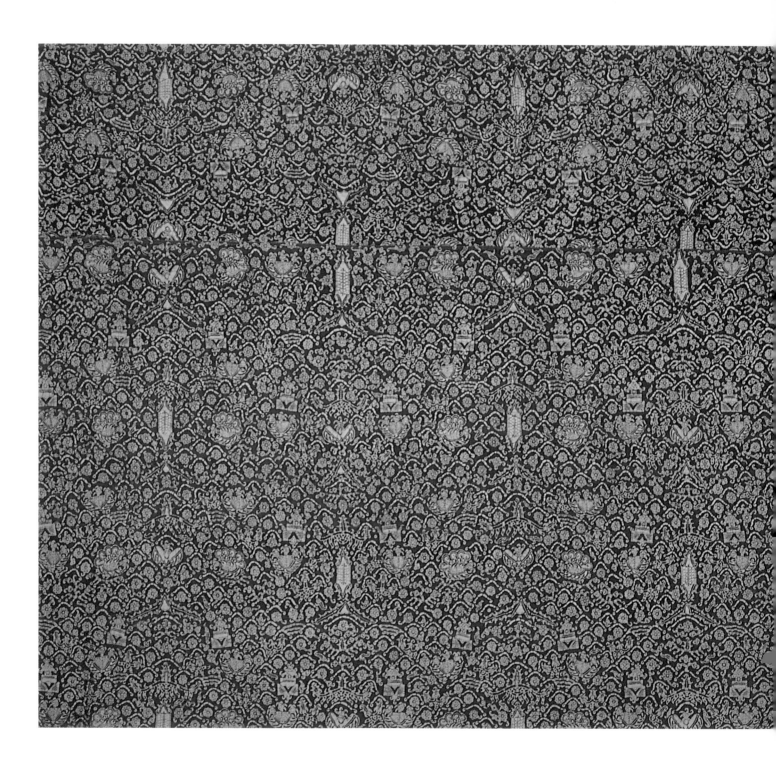

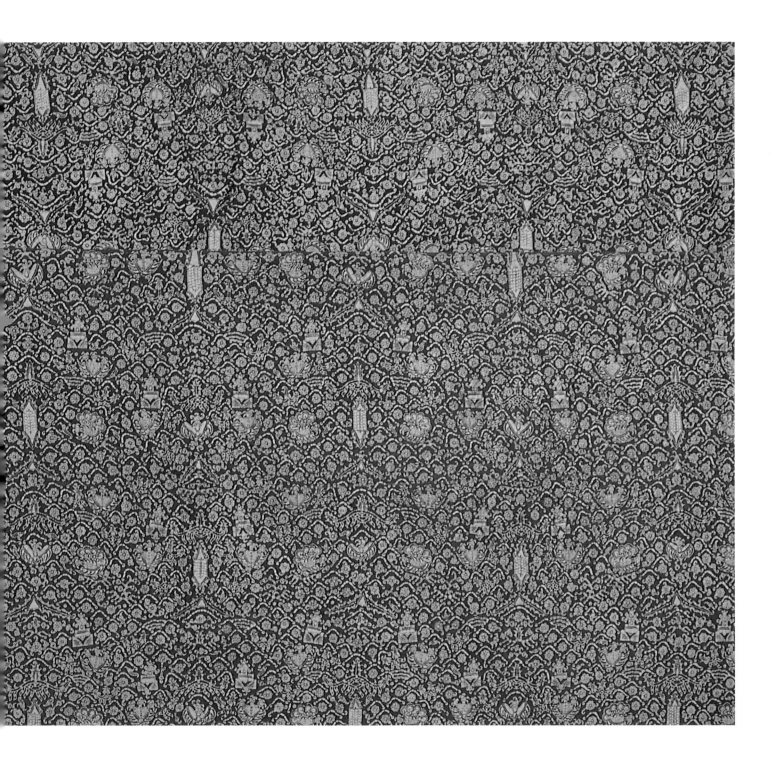

47

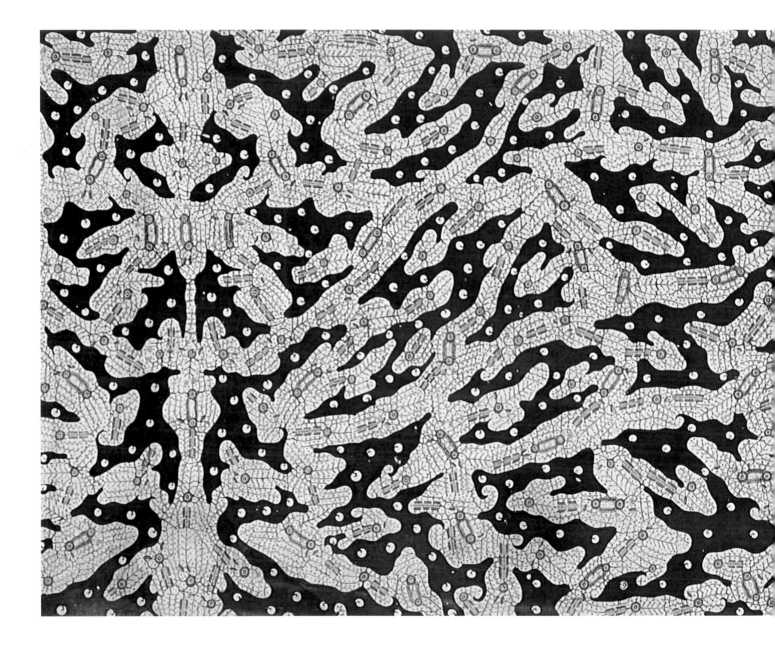

48

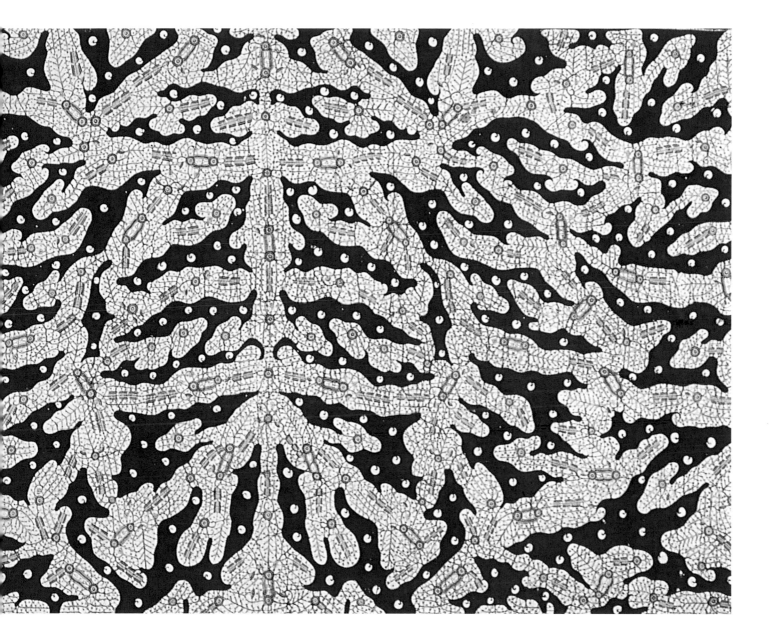

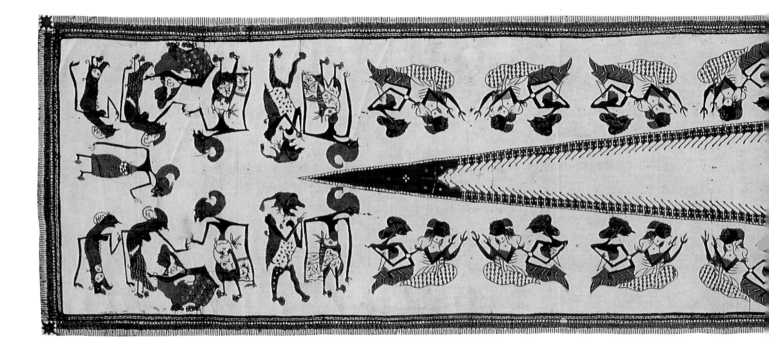

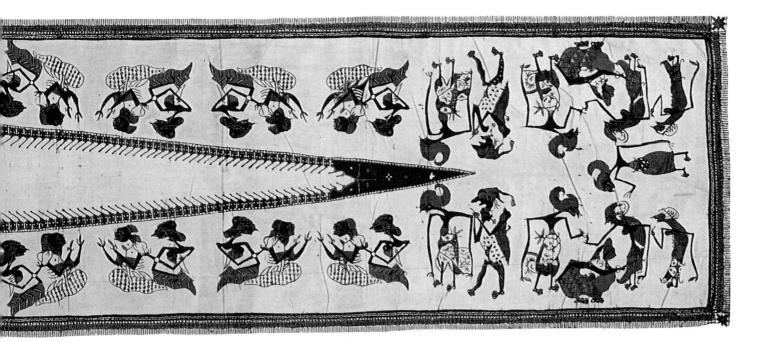

53

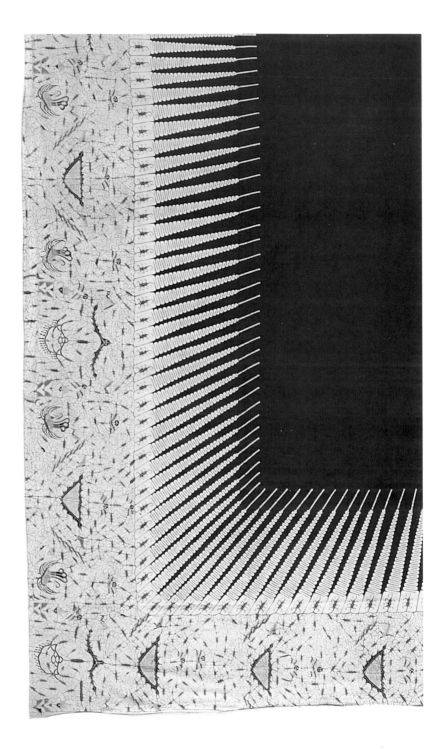

63

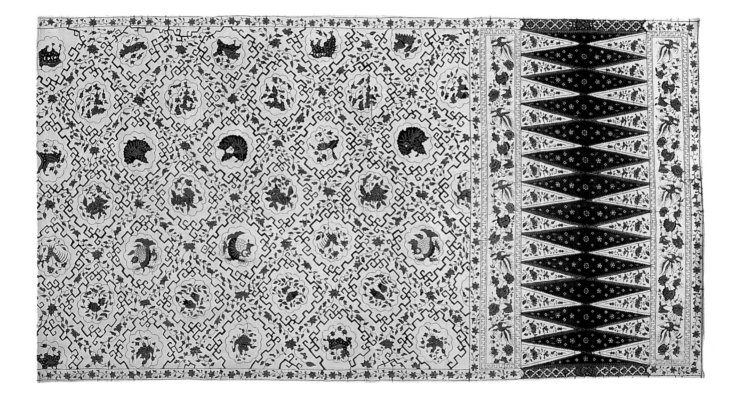

64

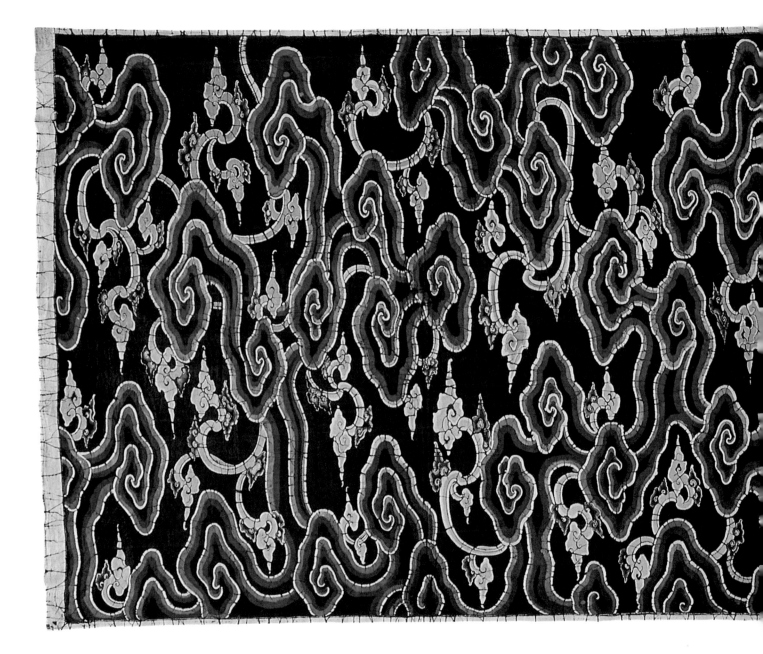

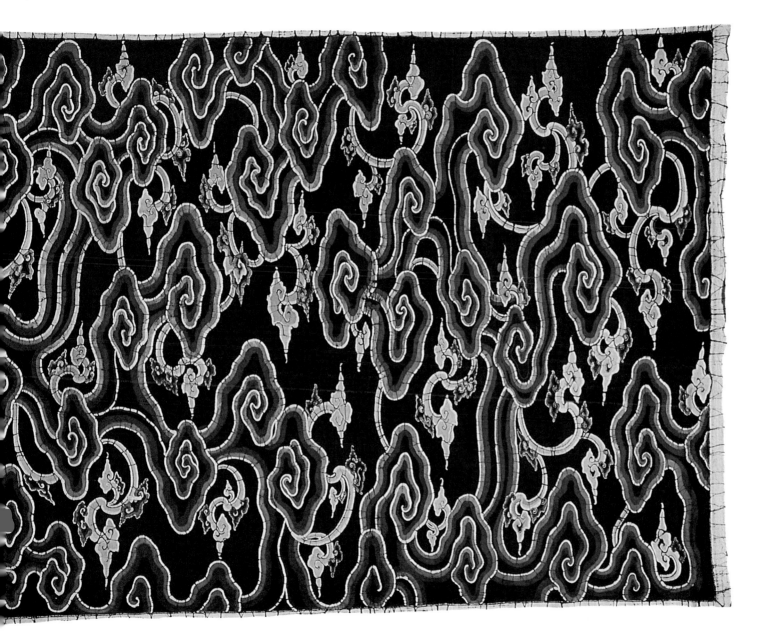

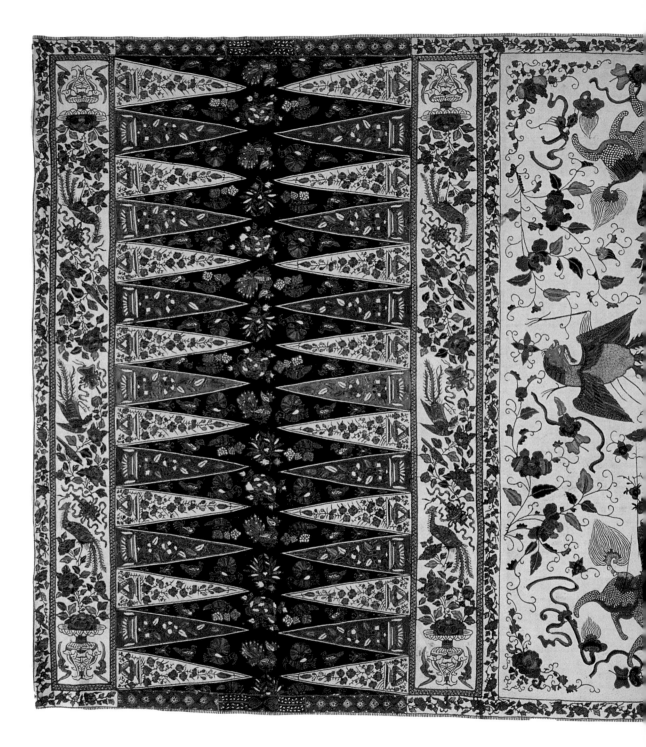

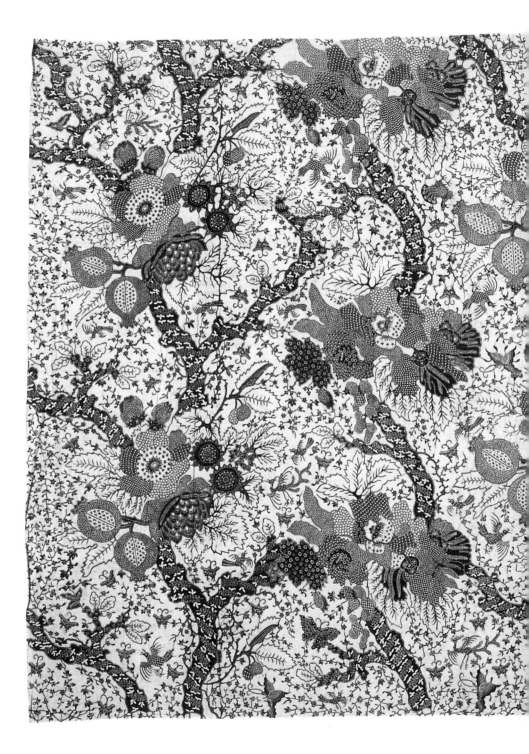

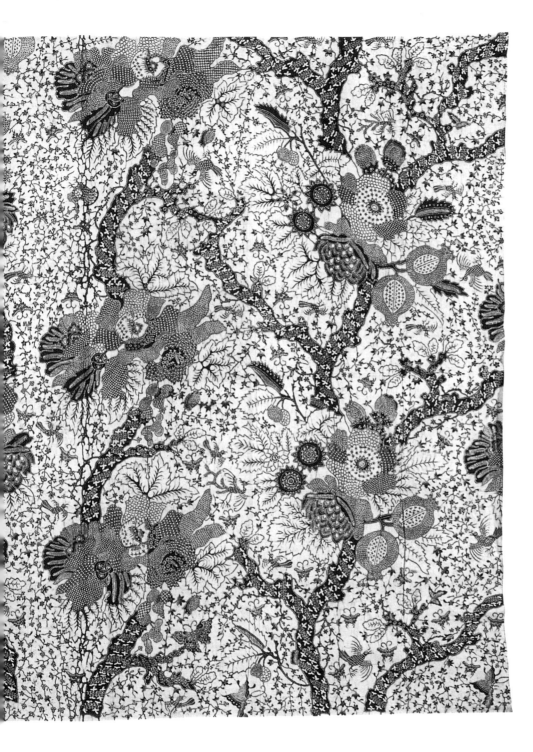

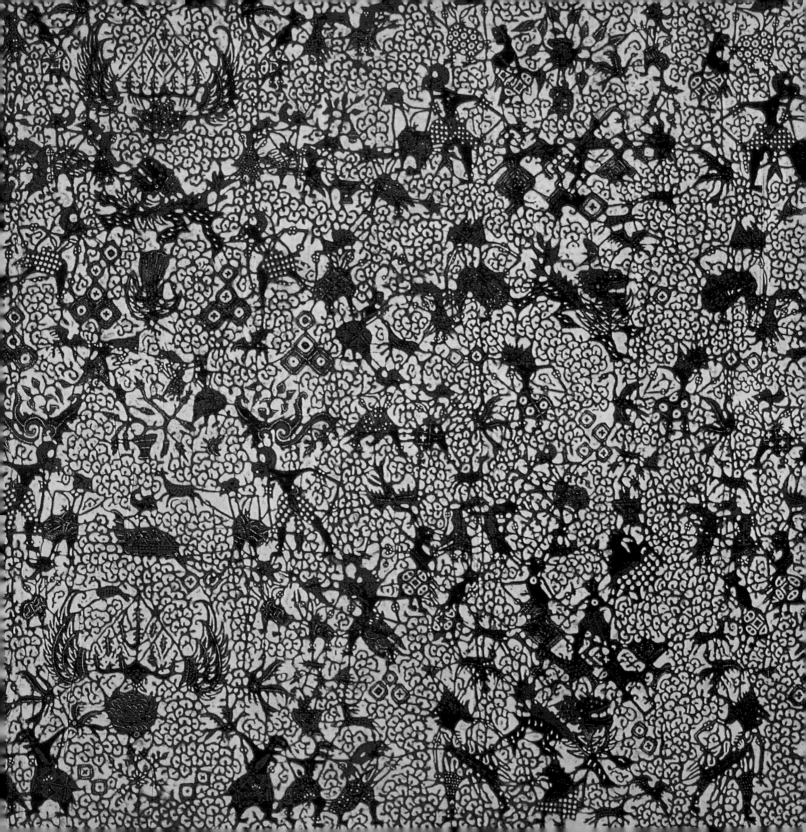

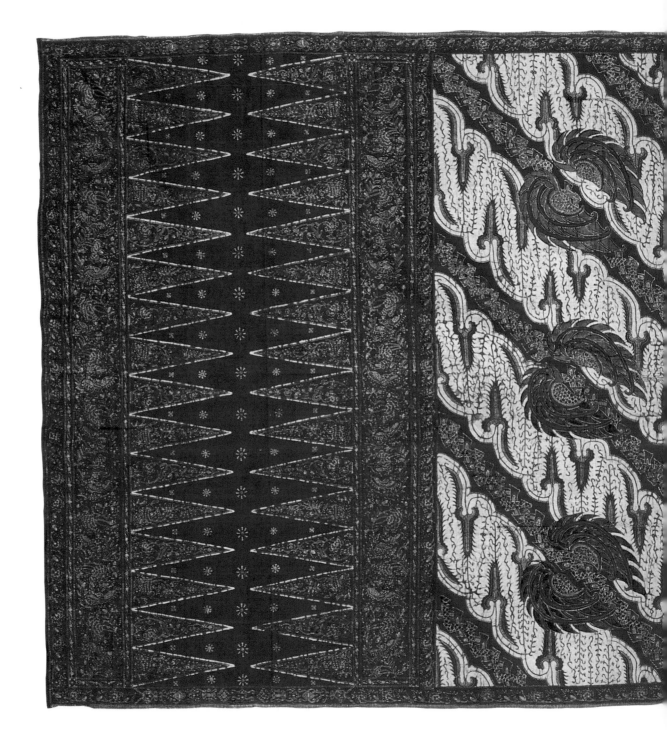

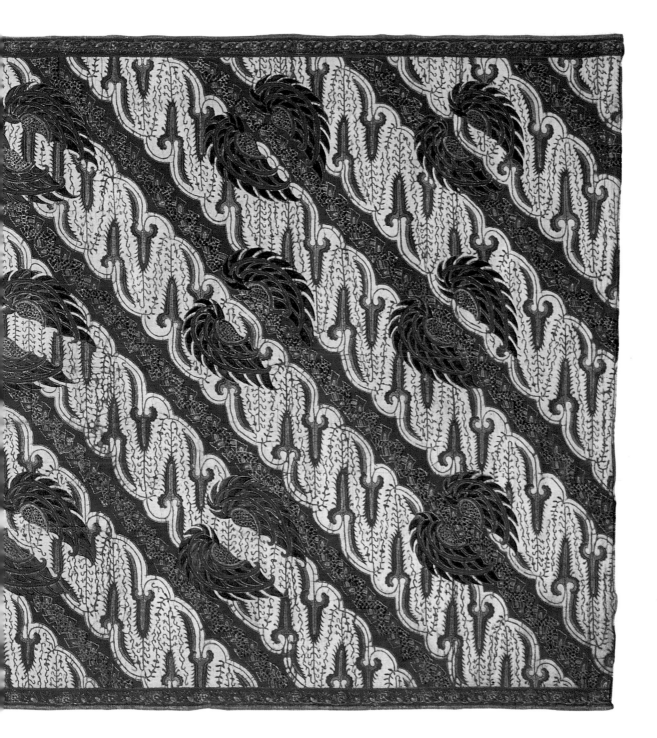

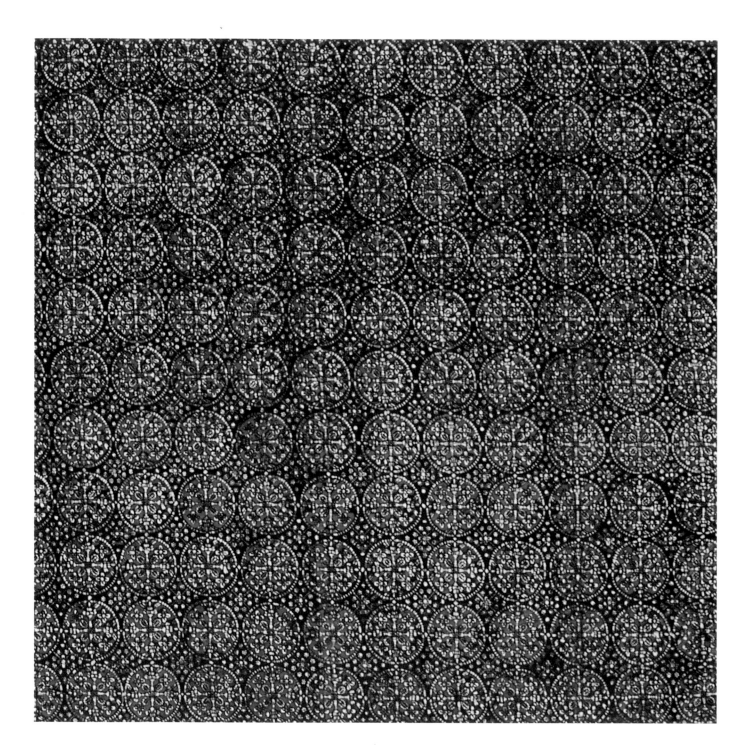

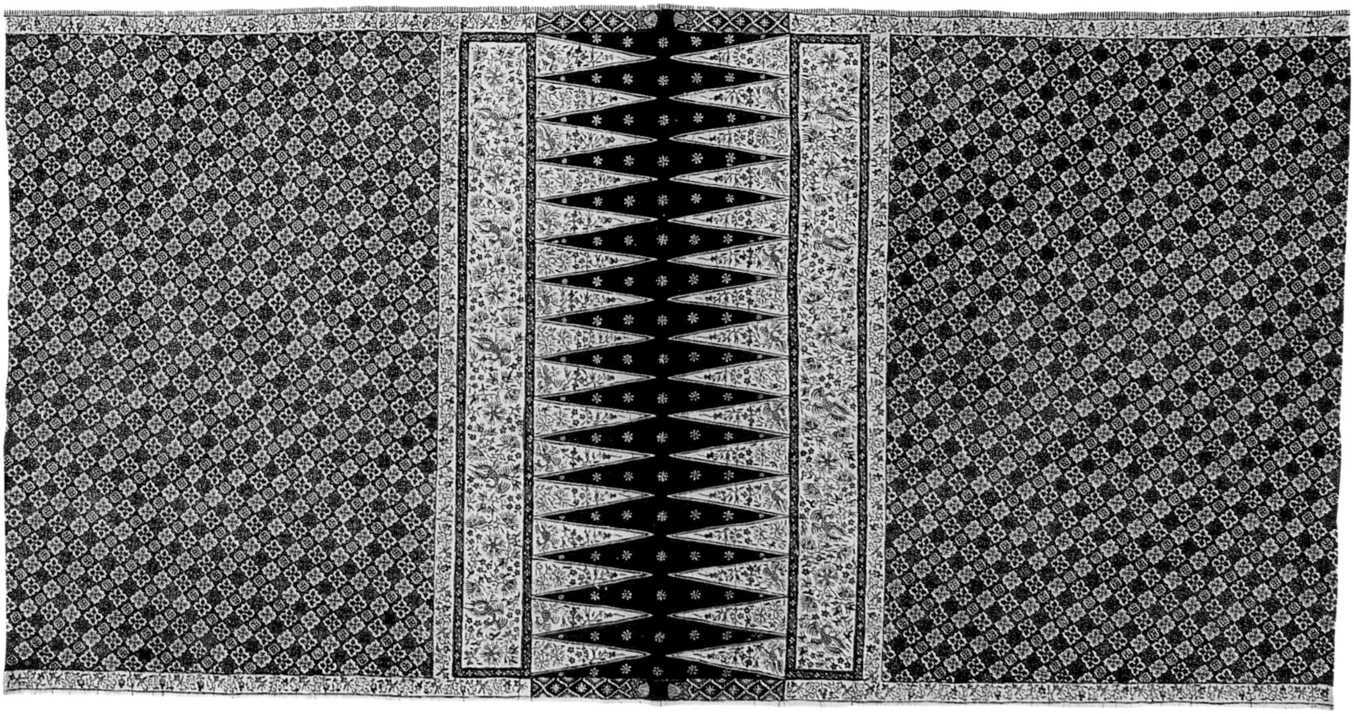

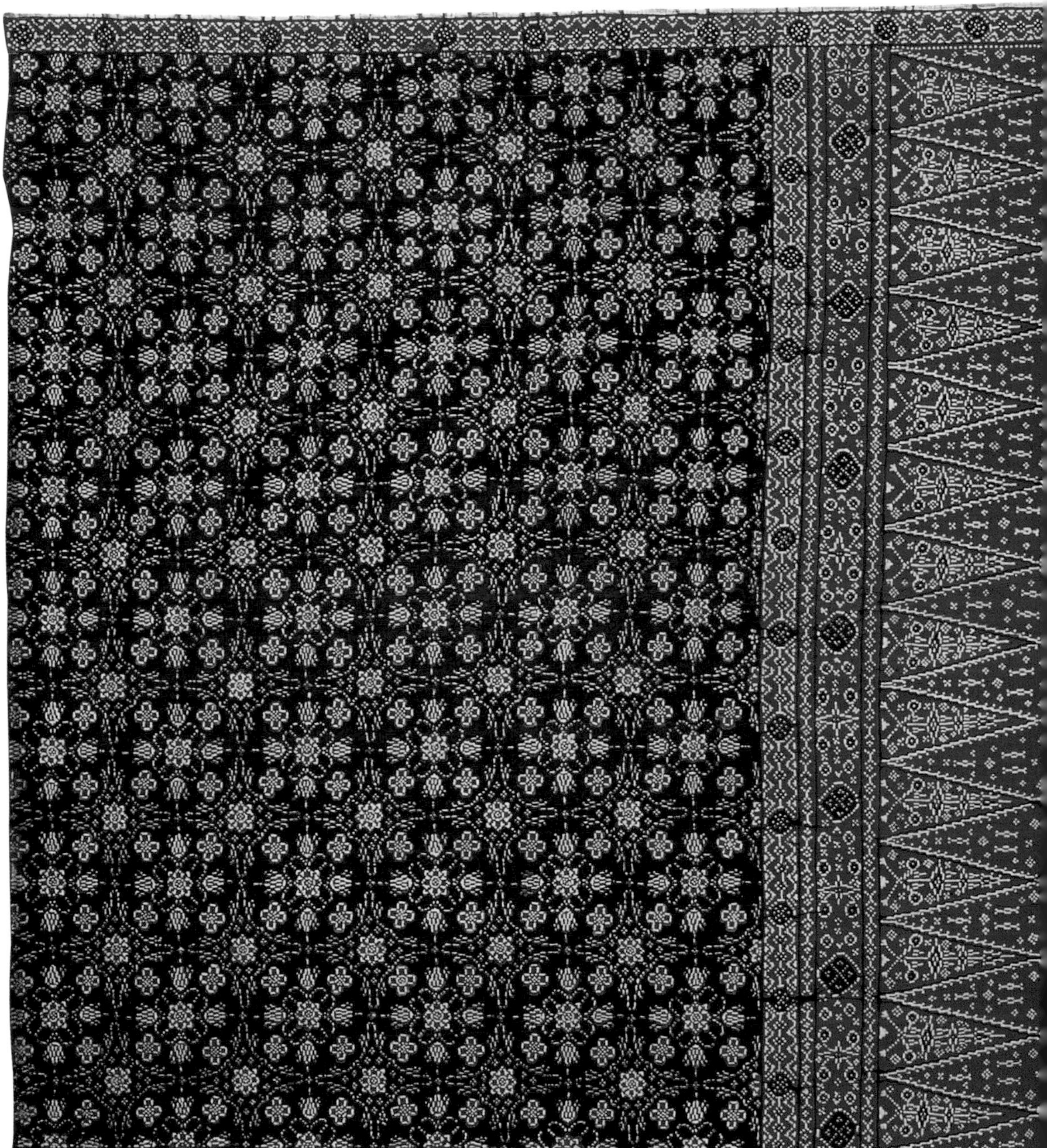

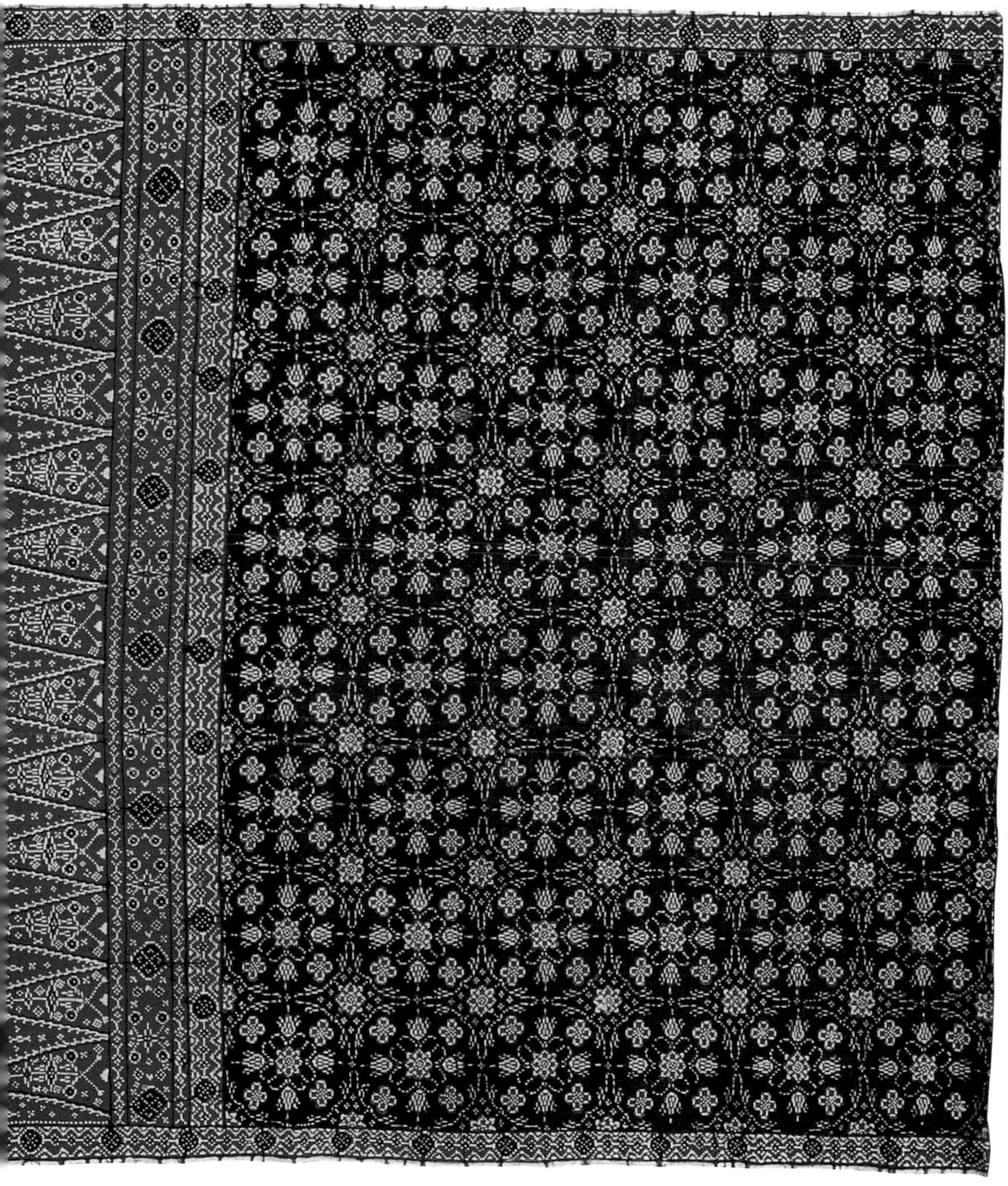

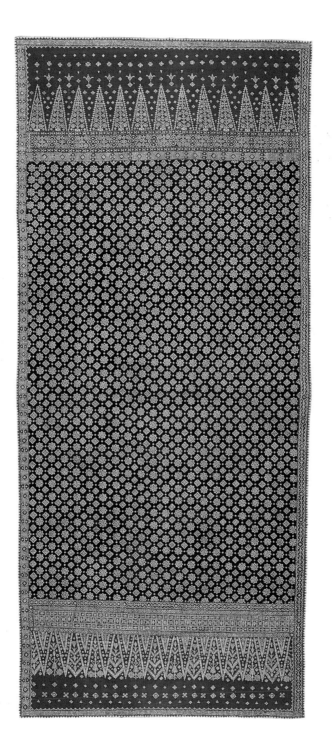

95

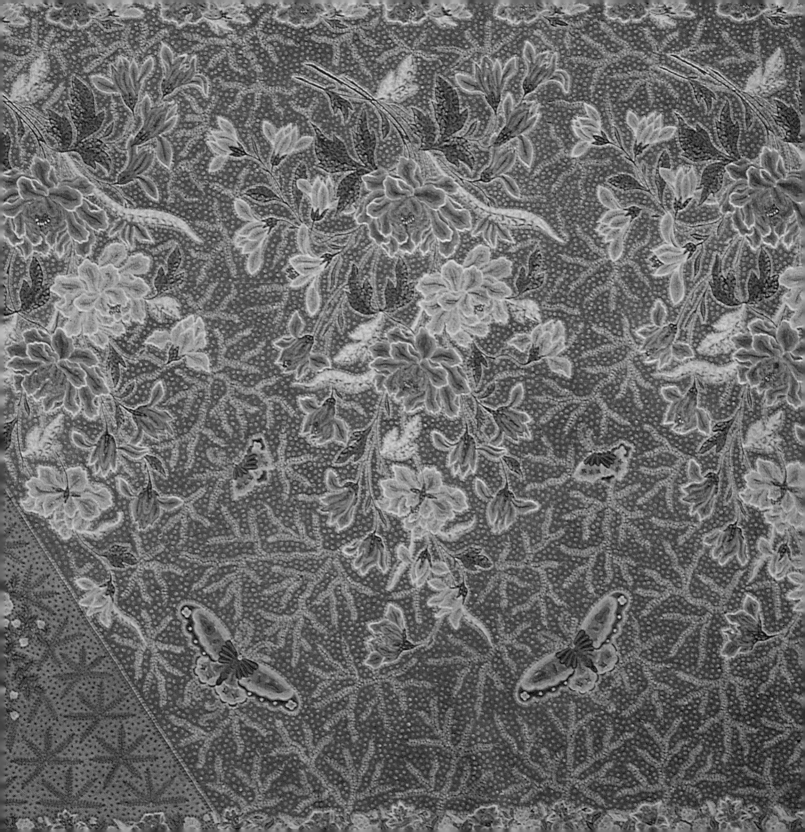

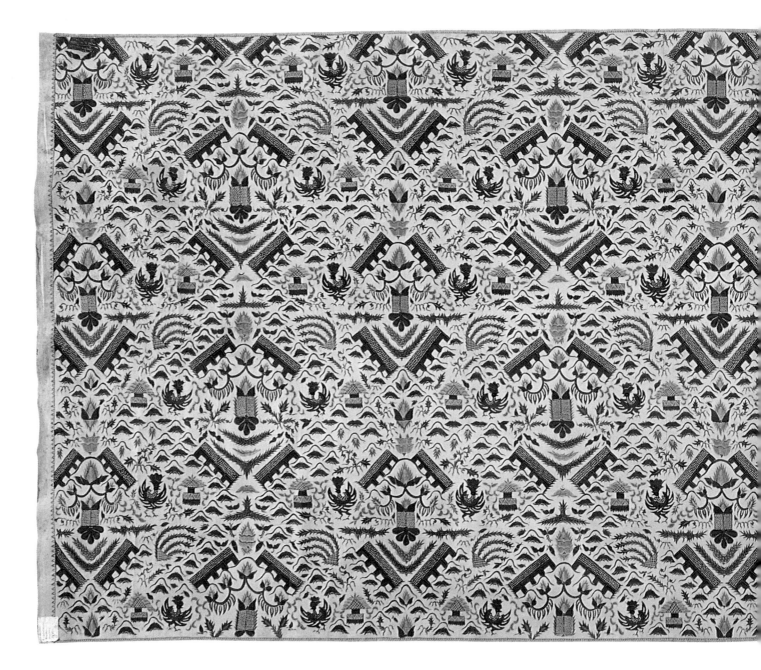

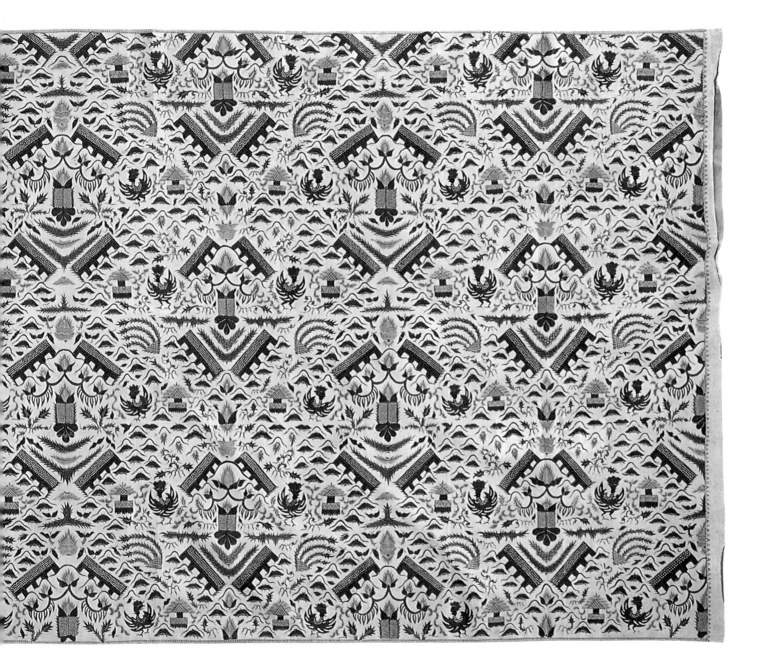

103

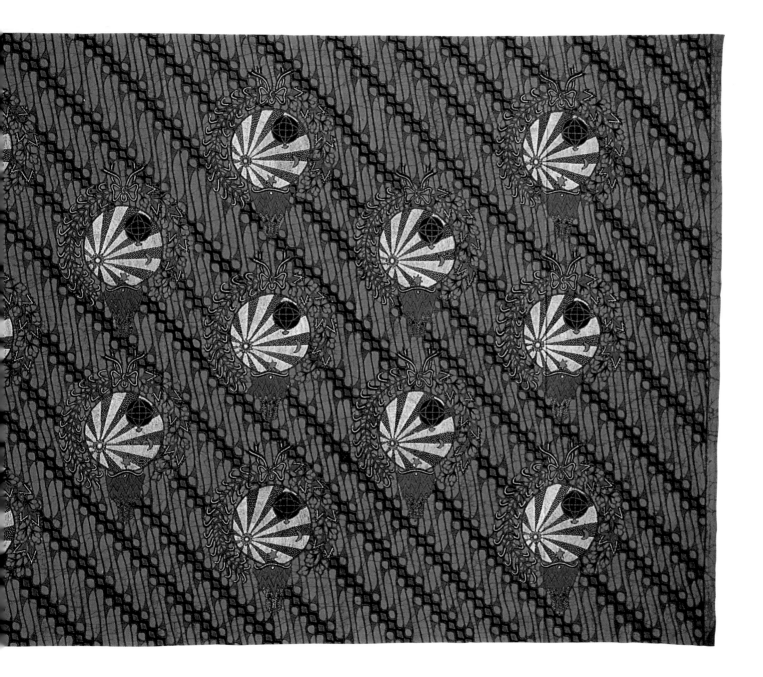

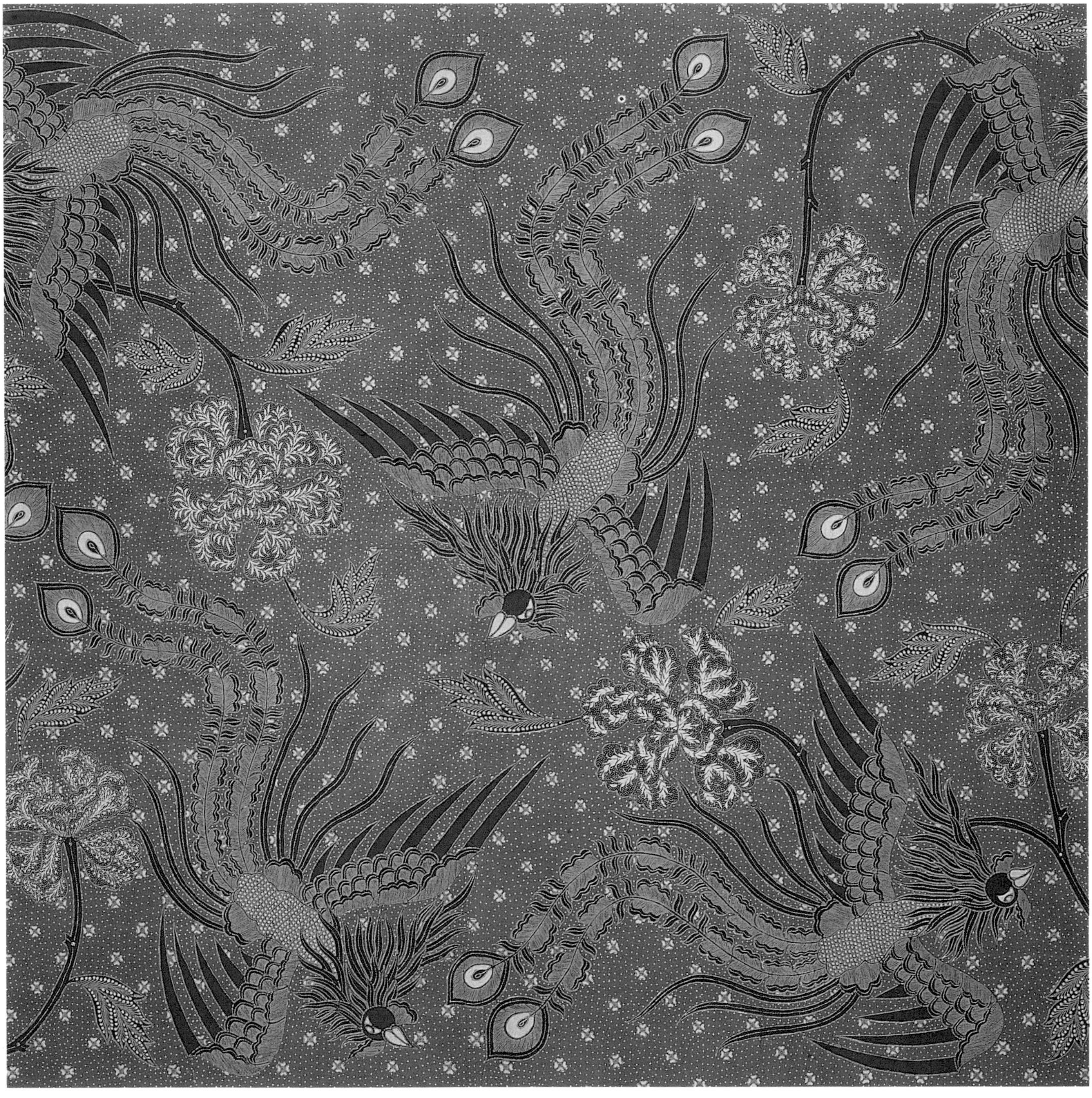